LOVE POEMS

Books by Anne Sexton

POETRY

To Bedlam and Part Way Back *1960*
All My Pretty Ones *1962*
Live or Die *1966*
Love Poems *1969*
Transformations *1971*
The Book of Folly *1972*
The Death Notebooks *1974*
The Awful Rowing Toward God *1975*
45 Mercy Street *1976*
Words for Dr. Y.: Uncollected Poems *1978*
The Complete Poems *1981*
Selected Poems of Anne Sexton *1988*

PROSE

Anne Sexton: A Self-Portrait in Letters *1977*

LOVE POEMS

Anne Sexton

FOREWORD BY
Diane Wood Middlebrook

A Mariner Book
HOUGHTON MIFFLIN COMPANY
BOSTON   NEW YORK

First Mariner Books edition 1999

Copyright © 1967, 1968, 1969 by Anne Sexton
Foreword copyright © 1989 by Diane Wood Middlebrook
All rights reserved

For information about permission to reproduce selections from
this book, write to Permissions, Houghton Mifflin Company,
215 Park Avenue South, New York, New York 10003.

Library of Congress Cataloging-in-Publication Data

Sexton, Anne.
Love poems / Anne Sexton ; foreword by
Diane Wood Middlebrook.
p.   cm.
ISBN 0-395-95777-X
1. Love poetry, American.   I. Title
PS3537.E915L6   1990   89-34994
811'.54—dc20   CIP

Printed in the United States of America

QUM 10 9 8 7 6 5 4 3 2

Some of the poems in this volume have previously appeared in
various magazines, as follows: *The Atlantic:* "You All Know the
Story of the Other Woman." Copyright © 1968 by The Atlantic
Monthly Company. *Audience:* "Just Once." Copyright © 1958 by
the Audience Press, Inc. *Critical Quarterly:* "The Breast" and
portions of "Eighteen Days Without You" (under the title "With
You Gone"). *Harper's Magazine:* "The Nude Swim." *The Hudson
Review,* Vol. XXI, No. 1 (Spring 1968): "The Interrogation of the
Man of Many Hearts," "The Break," "The Ballad of the Lonely
Masturbator." *New American Review:* "The Touch." *The New
Yorker:* "For My Lover, Returning to His Wife," "It Is a Spring
Afternoon," "Moon Song, Woman Song" (under the title "Moon
Song"), "Us," and portions of "Eighteen Days Without You"
(under the title "Days Without You"). *The Quarterly Review of
Literature:* "The Kiss," "In Celebration of My Uterus," "Song for
a Red Nightgown."

CONTENTS

FOREWORD

Anne Sexton's *Love Poems* gave American literature its first
fully sexual heroine. The speaker of Sexton's poems dwells
with husband and children in affluent, white Protestant
America just after the death of JFK. Her story begins after
the fairy-tale ending of "happily ever . . . ," begins in
the "post-pill paradise" of sexual revolution. More than a
century earlier, Hawthorne had created in *The Scarlet Let-
ter* a sexual female protagonist, Hester Prynne — to exhibit
her leading a life of disgrace at the margins of the town be-
cause of her sin of adultery. In Sexton's New England the
margins of town have been transformed into suburbia, and
adultery looms as the next horizon of sexual destiny, once
marriage and childbirth have ripened a woman's body and
mapped her pleasure centers. In 1969 this was new; no
woman had published such poems in English for centuries.

Adultery is the theme that gives *Love Poems* its serious-
ness and importance. Because it is at once transgressive and
banal, sensational and predictable, the love affair of a mar-
ried woman invites the powers of the storyteller. Sexton
was always a storyteller in her poetry; the titles of these
love poems mark, like the stars of a familiar constellation,
points of reference we can easily connect into a narrative.
"The Touch" leads on to "The Kiss," to "The Breast" —
and to hesitations: what manner of man is this "Man of
Many Hearts"? Consummations follow. The plot takes a
downward turn when the lover returns to his wife. Ensues
"The Break," the "Again and Again and Again" of pain,
"The Ballad of the Lonely Masturbator." Another cycle
opens: "Barefoot," "Now," "Us," "Mr. Mine"; then an-
other separation, the "Eighteen Days Without You."

Once through such a cycle might yield romance or trag-edy, but Sexton's love poems, taken together, tell another kind of story, complex and ambiguous. They trace the rise and fall and rise of the desire that, like a drug, awakens feeling and steals sense, brings transformation and addic-tion and sadness in the same dose. With a frankness new to the serious literature of her day, Sexton celebrates the sensual frontiers discoverable in the body of each new lover, man or woman, no two alike. There is lovely reso-nance to the sexual knowingness in many lines of these unmaidenly poems. Can adultery be heroic? Maybe not, but it can be spiritually educational. When the moment of consummation drains away, consciousness and conscience return, and that is why adultery rather than adult female sexuality is Sexton's theme. Adultery is still a sin in Sex-ton's book; it rubs against the grain of self-esteem, prompt-ing sober insights about the origins and significance of our most seductive illusions.

The love poems of Anne Sexton have an obvious literary cohort in the fictions of John Updike, whose *Couples* be-came a best seller during the months when Sexton was writing these poems: "post-pill paradise" was a phrase Up-dike put into the mouth of one of its characters, a liberated housewife. Sexton read the book and sent Updike a fan let-ter (a fan postcard, actually) after *Time* magazine featured him on the cover and ran a story titled "The Adulterous Society," with a review of *Couples* as its centerpiece. And *Love Poems* would become a kind of best seller, too: con-tinuously in print for twenty years, with nearly 100,000 copies sold.

But for all the many interesting similarities between Up-dike's fictions of the 1960s and Sexton's *Love Poems*, the perspective in Sexton's work is irreducibly womanly. Up-dike's female characters, however fastidiously rendered, come off as masculine projections: from the benignly self-absorbed to the sexual adepts among them, they are crea-tures of unreal consistency, fantasies. Many of Sexton's love poems are situated on the receiving end of just such fantasies; "The Touch" and "The Breast" offer some grotesque examples. Yes, her speaker is used to the feeling of dismemberment by the gaze of desire:

> Notice how he has numbered the blue veins
> in my breast. Moreover there are ten freckles.
> Now he goes left. Now he goes right.
> He is building a city, a city of flesh.
> He's an industrialist. He has starved in cellars
> and, ladies and gentlemen, he's been broken by iron,
> by the blood, by the metal, by the triumphant
> iron of his mother's death. But he begins again.
> Now he constructs me. . . .   ("Mr. Mine")

The broad ironies tell us this is foreplay, yet they also insert us disquietingly into a state of mind, an intelligence about the feelings of this object of desire: rigid while she is being figured out; and frigid? Within a page, though, comes "Knee Song," and a change of rhythm — short lines that fall as with catches of breath. Whoever or whatever is administering this polymorphous pleasure goes unidentified by gender or name. The point is, the female speaker in *Love Poems* has learned the frets and stops of her instrument, can play on it many a kind of tune.

Sexton herself had avoided publishing poems about love, for fear of being typecast as "lady poet." Of her first book, *To Bedlam and Part Way Back*, she gloated just before publication, "Not a love lyric in the lot." By 1969 she was an established poet, winner of a Pulitzer Prize, and she was a mature poet as well. The one piece she rescued for *Love Poems* from a discard pile ("Just Once") represents Sexton's earliest, most unsophisticated voice and broadens the range of feeling in *Love Poems*, sweetens the mixture with some old-fashioned sentiment.

The most ambitious poetry in this book comes last. In "Eighteen Days Without You," the frame of reference widens systematically from the exquisitely personal to the political, positioning the lovers' bodies in a social world. The year is 1966. Kennedy has been shot; other assassinations and catastrophes, as we know, wait their turn on the calendar and are foreshadowed in the poem, essential to the design of the sequence and to the design of the book. For "Eighteen Days" was composed under the influence of the evil star of Vietnam. Like most poets when confronted with a request for political poetry, Sexton had felt helpless and fraudulent in attempting to fashion humane sentiments for public consumption. Asked in 1968 for a contribution to a "Literary and Art Auction to support spring and summer actions against the war," Sexton released to the committee a manuscript of "The Touch," worrying that it didn't really seem appropriate. But the pressure to rise to this challenge probably clarified for her exactly what a poet could and could not do, as a poet, on behalf of peace. Her unpretentious artistic solution to the problem of bringing home the war was the poetic sequence "Eighteen Days." Its adulterous lovers are as guilty as anyone: safe, affluent, self-indulgent, ignorant of the worst things history is readying in the wings, and protected anyway by their ordinary privileges. Nor are they heroic: she knows they will grow bored with each other — "take a supper together and that / will be that." Against this cynicism the poem offers no argument, only images fashioned in praise of tenderness.

> We are bare. We are stripped to the bone
> and we swim in tandem and go up and up
> the river, the identical river called Mine
> and we enter together. No one's alone.

The simple, sure-footed language builds into the sequence a spiritual center at once personal and communal. If "Eighteen Days Without You" makes few claims as a stand against war, it does make a stand on behalf of feeling. It imagines difference melting into union. It meets standards by which we have always measured love poetry. And it is Anne Sexton at her best.

DIANE WOOD MIDDLEBROOK
1989

One should say before sleeping, "I have lived many lives. I have been a slave and a prince. Many a beloved has sat upon my knees and I have sat upon the knees of many a beloved. Everything that has been shall be again."

FROM AN ESSAY BY W. B. YEATS

The Touch

For months my hand had been sealed off
in a tin box. Nothing was there but subway railings.
Perhaps it is bruised, I thought,
and that is why they have locked it up.
But when I looked in it lay there quietly.
You could tell time by this, I thought,
like a clock, by its five knuckles
and the thin underground veins.
It lay there like an unconscious woman
fed by tubes she knew not of.

The hand had collapsed,
a small wood pigeon
that had gone into seclusion.
I turned it over and the palm was old,
its lines traced like fine needlepoint
and stitched up into the fingers.
It was fat and soft and blind in places.
Nothing but vulnerable.

And all this is metaphor.
An ordinary hand — just lonely
for something to touch
that touches back.
The dog won't do it.
Her tail wags in the swamp for a frog.
I'm no better than a case of dog food.
She owns her own hunger.
My sisters won't do it.
They live in school except for buttons
and tears running down like lemonade.

My father won't do it.
He comes with the house and even at night
he lives in a machine made by my mother
and well oiled by his job, his job.

The trouble is
that I'd let my gestures freeze.
The trouble was not
in the kitchen or the tulips
but only in my head, my head.

Then all this became history.
Your hand found mine.
Life rushed to my fingers like a blood clot.
Oh, my carpenter,
the fingers are rebuilt.
They dance with yours.
They dance in the attic and in Vienna.
My hand is alive all over America.
Not even death will stop it,
death shedding her blood.
Nothing will stop it, for this is the kingdom
and the kingdom come.

The Kiss

My mouth blooms like a cut.
I've been wronged all year, tedious
nights, nothing but rough elbows in them
and delicate boxes of Kleenex calling *crybaby
crybaby, you fool!*

Before today my body was useless.
Now it's tearing at its square corners.
It's tearing old Mary's garments off, knot by knot
and see — Now it's shot full of these electric bolts.
Zing! A resurrection!

Once it was a boat, quite wooden
and with no business, no salt water under it
and in need of some paint. It was no more
than a group of boards. But you hoisted her, rigged her.
She's been elected.

My nerves are turned on. I hear them like
musical instruments. Where there was silence
the drums, the strings are incurably playing. You did this.
Pure genius at work. Darling, the composer has stepped
into fire.

The Breast

This is the key to it.
This is the key to everything.
Preciously.

I am worse than the gamekeeper's children,
picking for dust and bread.
Here I am drumming up perfume.

Let me go down on your carpet,
your straw mattress — whatever's at hand
because the child in me is dying, dying.

It is not that I am cattle to be eaten.
It is not that I am some sort of street.
But your hands found me like an architect.

Jugful of milk! It was yours years ago
when I lived in the valley of my bones,
bones dumb in the swamp. Little playthings.

A xylophone maybe with skin
stretched over it awkwardly.
Only later did it become something real.

Later I measured my size against movie stars.
I didn't measure up. Something between
my shoulders was there. But never enough.

Sure, there was a meadow,
but no young men singing the truth.
Nothing to tell truth by.

Ignorant of men I lay next to my sisters
and rising out of the ashes I cried
my sex will be transfixed!

Now I am your mother, your daughter,
your brand new thing — a snail, a nest.
I am alive when your fingers are.

I wear silk — the cover to uncover —
because silk is what I want you to think of.
But I dislike the cloth. It is too stern.

So tell me anything but track me like a climber
for here is the eye, here is the jewel,
here is the excitement the nipple learns.

I am unbalanced — but I am not mad with snow.
I am mad the way young girls are mad,
with an offering, an offering . . .

I burn the way money burns.

The Interrogation of
the Man of Many Hearts

Who's she,
that one in your arms?

She's the one I carried my bones to
and built a house that was just a cot
and built a life that was over an hour
and built a castle where no one lives
and built, in the end, a song
to go with the ceremony.

Why have you brought her here?
Why do you knock on my door
with your little stories and songs?

I had joined her the way a man joins
a woman and yet there was no place
for festivities or formalities
and these things matter to a woman
and, you see, we live in a cold climate
and are not permitted to kiss on the street
so I made up a song that wasn't true.
I made up a song called *Marriage.*

You come to me out of wedlock
and kick your foot on my stoop
and ask me to measure such things?

Never. Never. Not my real wife.
She's my real witch, my fork, my mare,
my mother of tears, my skirtful of hell,
the stamp of my sorrows, the stamp of my bruises
and also the children she might bear

and also a private place, a body of bones
that I would honestly buy, if I could buy,
that I would marry, if I could marry.

And should I torment you for that?
Each man has a small fate allotted to him
and yours is a passionate one.

But I am in torment. We have no place.
The cot we share is almost a prison
where I can't say buttercup, bobolink,
sugarduck, pumpkin, love ribbon, locket,
valentine, summergirl, funnygirl and all
those nonsense things one says in bed.
To say I have bedded with her is not enough.
I have not only bedded her down.
I have tied her down with a knot.

Then why do you stick your fists
into your pockets? Why do you shuffle
your feet like a schoolboy?

For years I have tied this knot in my dreams.
I have walked through a door in my dreams
and she was standing there in my mother's apron.
Once she crawled through a window that was shaped
like a keyhole and she was wearing my daughter's
pink corduroys and each time I tied these women
in a knot. Once a queen came. I tied her too.
But this is something I have actually tied
and now I have made her fast.
I sang her out. I caught her down.
I stamped her out with a song.

There was no other apartment for it.
There was no other chamber for it.
Only the knot. The bedded-down knot.
Thus I have laid my hands upon her
and have called her eyes and her mouth
as mine, and also her tongue.

Why do you ask me to make choices?
I am not a judge or a psychologist.
You own your bedded-down knot.

And yet I have real daytimes and nighttimes
with children and balconies and a good wife.
Thus I have tied these other knots,
yet I would rather not think of them
when I speak to you of her. Not now.
If she were a room to rent I would pay.
If she were a life to save I would save.
Maybe I am a man of many hearts.

A man of many hearts?
Why then do you tremble at my doorway?
A man of many hearts does not need me.

I'm caught deep in the dye of her.
I have allowed you to catch me red-handed,
catch me with my wild oats in a wild clock
for my mare, my dove and my own clean body.
People might say I have snakes in my boots
but I tell you that just once am I in the stirrups,
just once, this once, in the cup.
The love of the woman is in the song.
I called her the woman in red.
I called her the girl in pink

but she was ten colors
and ten women.
I could hardly name her.

I know who she is.
You have named her enough.

Maybe I shouldn't have put it in words.
Frankly, I think I'm worse for this kissing,
drunk as a piper, kicking the traces
and determined to tie her up forever.
You see the song is the life,
the life I can't live.
God, even as he passes,
hands down monogamy like slang.
I wanted to write her into the law.
But, you know, there is no law for this.

Man of many hearts, you are a fool!
The clover has grown thorns this year
and robbed the cattle of their fruit
and the stones of the river
have sucked men's eyes dry,
season after season,
and every bed has been condemned,
not by morality or law,
but by time.

That Day

This is the desk I sit at
and this is the desk where I love you too much
and this is the typewriter that sits before me
where yesterday only your body sat before me
with its shoulders gathered in like a Greek chorus,
with its tongue like a king making up rules as he goes,
with its tongue quite openly like a cat lapping milk,
with its tongue — both of us coiled in its slippery life.
That was yesterday, that day.

That was the day of your tongue,
your tongue that came from your lips,
two openers, half animals, half birds
caught in the doorway of your heart.
That was the day I followed the king's rules,
passing by your red veins and your blue veins,
my hands down the backbone, down quick like a firepole,
hands between legs where you display your inner
      knowledge,
where diamond mines are buried and come forth to bury,
come forth more sudden than some reconstructed city.
It is complete within seconds, that monument.
The blood runs underground yet brings forth a tower.
A multitude should gather for such an edifice.
For a miracle one stands in line and throws confetti.
Surely The Press is here looking for headlines.
Surely someone should carry a banner on the sidewalk.
If a bridge is constructed doesn't the mayor cut a ribbon?
If a phenomenon arrives shouldn't the Magi come bearing
      gifts?
Yesterday was the day I bore gifts for your gift
and came from the valley to meet you on the pavement.
That was yesterday, that day.

That was the day of your face,
your face after love, close to the pillow, a lullaby.
Half asleep beside me letting the old fashioned rocker stop,
our breath became one, became a child-breath together,
while my fingers drew little o's on your shut eyes,
while my fingers drew little smiles on your mouth,
while I drew I LOVE YOU on your chest and its drummer
and whispered, "Wake up!" and you mumbled in your
        sleep,
"Sh. We're driving to Cape Cod. We're heading for the
        Bourne
Bridge. We're circling around the Bourne Circle." Bourne!
Then I knew you in your dream and prayed of our time
that I would be pierced and you would take root in me
and that I might bring forth your born, might bear
the you or the ghost of you in my little household.
Yesterday I did not want to be borrowed
but this is the typewriter that sits before me
and love is where yesterday is at.

In Celebration of My Uterus

Everyone in me is a bird.
I am beating all my wings.
They wanted to cut you out
but they will not.
They said you were immeasurably empty
but you are not.
They said you were sick unto dying
but they were wrong.
You are singing like a school girl.
You are not torn.

Sweet weight,
in celebration of the woman I am
and of the soul of the woman I am
and of the central creature and its delight
I sing for you. I dare to live.
Hello, spirit. Hello, cup.
Fasten, cover. Cover that does contain.
Hello to the soil of the fields.
Welcome, roots.

Each cell has a life.
There is enough here to please a nation.
It is enough that the populace own these goods.
Any person, any commonwealth would say of it,
"It is good this year that we may plant again
and think forward to a harvest.
A blight had been forecast and has been cast out."
Many women are singing together of this:
one is in a shoe factory cursing the machine,
one is at the aquarium tending a seal,
one is dull at the wheel of her Ford,
one is at the toll gate collecting,
one is tying the cord of a calf in Arizona,

one is straddling a cello in Russia,
one is shifting pots on the stove in Egypt,
one is painting her bedroom walls moon color,
one is dying but remembering a breakfast,
one is stretching on her mat in Thailand,
one is wiping the ass of her child,
one is staring out the window of a train
in the middle of Wyoming and one is
anywhere and some are everywhere and all
seem to be singing, although some can not
sing a note.

Sweet weight,
in celebration of the woman I am
let me carry a ten-foot scarf,
let me drum for the nineteen-year-olds,
let me carry bowls for the offering
(if that is my part).
Let me study the cardiovascular tissue,
let me examine the angular distance of meteors,
let me suck on the stems of flowers
(if that is my part).
Let me make certain tribal figures
(if that is my part).
For this thing the body needs
let me sing
for the supper,
for the kissing,
for the correct
yes.

The Nude Swim

On the southwest side of Capri
we found a little unknown grotto
where no people were and we
entered it completely
and let our bodies lose all
their loneliness.

All the fish in us
had escaped for a minute.
The real fish did not mind.
We did not disturb their personal life.
We calmly trailed over them
and under them, shedding
air bubbles, little white
balloons that drifted up
into the sun by the boat
where the Italian boatman slept
with his hat over his face.

Water so clear you could
read a book through it.
Water so buoyant you could
float on your elbow.
I lay on it as on a divan.
I lay on it just like
Matisse's *Red Odalisque*.
Water was my strange flower.
One must picture a woman
without a toga or a scarf
on a couch as deep as a tomb.

The walls of that grotto
were everycolor blue and
you said, "Look! Your eyes
are seacolor. Look! Your eyes
are skycolor." And my eyes
shut down as if they were
suddenly ashamed.

Song for a Red Nightgown

No. Not really red,
but the color of a rose when it bleeds.
It's a lost flamingo,
called somewhere Schiaparelli Pink
but not meaning pink, but blood and
those candy store cinnamon hearts.
It moves like capes in the unflawed
villages in Spain. Meaning a fire
layer and underneath, like a petal,
a sheath of pink, clean as a stone.

So I mean a nightgown of two colors
and of two layers that float from
the shoulders across every zone.
For years the moth has longed for them
but these colors are bounded by silence
and animals, half hidden but browsing.
One could think of feathers and
not know it at all. One could
think of whores and not imagine
the way of a swan. One could
imagine the cloth of a bee and
touch its hair and come close.

The bed is ravaged by such
sweet sights. The girl is.
The girl drifts up out of
her nightgown and its color.
Her wings are fastened onto
her shoulders like bandages.
The butterfly owns her now.
It covers her and her wounds.
She is not terrified of

begonias or telegrams but
surely this nightgown girl,
this awesome flyer, has not seen
how the moon floats through her
and in between.

Loving the Killer

Today is the day they shipped
home our summer in two crates
and tonight is All Hallows Eve
and today you tell me the oak leaves
outside your office window will
outlast the New England winter.
But then, love is where our summer
was.

Though I never touched a rifle,
love was under the canvas,
deep in the bush of Tanzania.
Though I only carried a camera,
love came after the gun,
after the kill,
after the martinis and
the eating of the kill.
While Saedi, a former cannibal,
served from the left
in his white gown and red fez,
I vomited behind the dining tent.
Love where the hyena laughed
in the middle of nowhere
except the equator. Love!

Yet today our dog is full
of our dead dog's spirit
and limps on three legs,
holding up the dead dog's paw.
Though the house is full of
candy bars the wasted ghost
of my parents is poking
the keyhole, rubbing the bedpost.
Also the ghost of your father,

who was killed outright.
Tonight we will argue and shout,
"My loss is greater than yours!
My pain is more valuable!"

Today they shipped home our summer
in two crates wrapped in brown
waxed paper and sewn in burlap.
The first crate holds our personal
effects, sweaty jackets, 3 lb. boots
from the hold of the S.S. *Mormacrio*
by way of Mombasa, Dar es Salaam,
Tanga, Lourenço Marques and Zanzibar,
through customs along with the other
merchandise: ash blonde sisal like
horses' tails, and hairy strings,
bales of grease wool from the auctions
at Cape Town and something else. Bones!

Bones piled up like coal, animal bones
shaped like golf balls, school pencils,
fingers and noses. Oh my Nazi,
with your S.S. sky-blue eye —
I am no different from Emily Goering.
Emily Goering recently said she
thought the concentration camps
were for the re-education of Jews
and Communists. She thought!
So far the continents stay on the map
but there is always a new method.

The other crate we own is dead.
Bones and skins from Hold #1
going to New York for curing and

mounting. We have not touched these
skulls since a Friday in Arusha where
skulls lay humbly beside the Land Rover,
flies still sucking on eye pits,
all in a row, head by head,
beside the ivory that cost more
than your life. The wildebeest
skull, the eland skull, the Grant's
skull, the Thomson's skull, the impala
skull and the hartebeest skull,
on and on to New York along with
the skins of zebras and leopards.

And tonight our skins, our bones,
that have survived our fathers,
will meet, delicate in the hold,
fastened together in an intricate
lock. Then one of us will shout,
"My need is more desperate!" and
I will eat you slowly with kisses
even though the killer in you
has gotten out.

For My Lover,
Returning to His Wife

She is all there.
She was melted carefully down for you
and cast up from your childhood,
cast up from your one hundred favorite aggies.

She has always been there, my darling.
She is, in fact, exquisite.
Fireworks in the dull middle of February
and as real as a cast-iron pot.

Let's face it, I have been momentary.
A luxury. A bright red sloop in the harbor.
My hair rising like smoke from the car window.
Littleneck clams out of season.

She is more than that. She is your have to have,
has grown you your practical your tropical growth.
This is not an experiment. She is all harmony.
She sees to oars and oarlocks for the dinghy,

has placed wild flowers at the window at breakfast,
sat by the potter's wheel at midday,
set forth three children under the moon,
three cherubs drawn by Michelangelo,

done this with her legs spread out
in the terrible months in the chapel.
If you glance up, the children are there
like delicate balloons resting on the ceiling.

She has also carried each one down the hall
after supper, their heads privately bent,
two legs protesting, person to person,
her face flushed with a song and their little sleep.

I give you back your heart.
I give you permission —

for the fuse inside her, throbbing
angrily in the dirt, for the bitch in her
and the burying of her wound —
for the burying of her small red wound alive —

for the pale flickering flare under her ribs,
for the drunken sailor who waits in her left pulse,
for the mother's knee, for the stockings,
for the garter belt, for the call —

the curious call
when you will burrow in arms and breasts
and tug at the orange ribbon in her hair
and answer the call, the curious call.

She is so naked and singular.
She is the sum of yourself and your dream.
Climb her like a monument, step after step.
She is solid.

As for me, I am a watercolor.
I wash off.

The Break

It was also my violent heart that broke,
falling down the front hall stairs.
It was also a message I never spoke,
calling, riser after riser, *who cares*

about you, who cares, splintering up
the hip that was merely made of crystal,
the post of it and also the cup.
I exploded in the hallway like a pistol.

So I fell apart. So I came all undone.
Yes. I was like a box of dog bones.
But now they've wrapped me in like a nun.
Burst like firecrackers! Held like stones!

What a feat sailing queerly like Icarus
until the tempest undid me and I broke.
The ambulance drivers made such a fuss.
But when I cried, "Wait for my courage!" they smoked

and then they placed me, tied me up on their plate,
and wheeled me out to their coffin, my nest.
Slowly the siren, slowly the hearse, sedate
as a dowager. At the E.W. they cut off my dress.

I cried, "Oh Jesus, help me! Oh Jesus Christ!"
and the nurse replied, "Wrong name. My name
is Barbara," and hung me in an odd device,
a buck's extension and a Balkan overhead frame.

The orthopedic man declared,
"You'll be down for a year." His scoop. His news.
He opened the skin. He scraped. He pared
and drilled through bone for his four-inch screws.

That takes brute strength like pushing a cow
up hill. I tell you, it takes skill
and bedside charm and all that know how.
The body is a damn hard thing to kill.

But please don't touch or jiggle my bed.
I'm Ethan Frome's wife. I'll move when I'm able.
The T.V. hangs from the wall like a moose head.
I hide a pint of bourbon in my bedside table.

A bird full of bones, now I'm held by a sand bag.
The fracture was twice. The fracture was double.
The days are horizontal. The days are a drag.
All of the skeleton in me is in trouble.

Across the hall is the bedpan station.
The urine and stools pass hourly by my head
in silver bowls. They flush in unison
in the autoclave. My one dozen roses are dead.

They have ceased to menstruate. They hang
there like little dried up blood clots.
And the heart too, that cripple, how it sang
once. How it thought it could call the shots!

Understand what happened the day that I fell.
My heart had stammered and hungered at
a marriage feast until the angel of hell
turned me into the punisher, the acrobat.

My bones are loose as clothespins,
as abandoned as dolls in a toy shop
and my heart, old hunger motor, with its sins
revved up like an engine that would not stop.

And now I spend all day taking care
of my body, that baby. Its cargo is scarred.
I anoint the bedpan. I brush my hair,
waiting in the pain machine for my bones to get hard,

for the soft, soft bones that were laid apart
and were screwed together. They will knit.
And the other corpse, the fractured heart,
I feed it piecemeal, little chalice. I'm good to it.

Yet like a fire alarm it waits to be known.
It is wired. In it many colors are stored.
While my body's in prison, heart cells alone
have multiplied. My bones are merely bored

with all this waiting around. But the heart,
this child of myself that resides in the flesh,
this ultimate signature of the me, the start
of my blindness and sleep, builds a death crèche.

The figures are placed at the grave of my bones.
All figures knowing it is the other death
they came for. Each figure standing alone.
The heart burst with love and lost its breath.

This little town, this little country is real
and thus it is so of the post and the cup
and thus of the violent heart. The zeal
of my house doth eat me up.

It Is a Spring Afternoon

Everything here is yellow and green.
Listen to its throat, its earthskin,
the bone dry voices of the peepers
as they throb like advertisements.
The small animals of the woods
are carrying their deathmasks
into a narrow winter cave.
The scarecrow has plucked out
his two eyes like diamonds
and walked into the village.
The general and the postman
have taken off their packs.
This has all happened before
but nothing here is obsolete.
Everything here is possible.

Because of this
perhaps a young girl has laid down
her winter clothes and has casually
placed herself upon a tree limb
that hangs over a pool in the river.
She has been poured out onto the limb,
low above the houses of the fishes
as they swim in and out of her reflection
and up and down the stairs of her legs.
Her body carries clouds all the way home.
She is overlooking her watery face
in the river where blind men
come to bathe at midday.
Because of this
the ground, that winter nightmare,
has cured its sores and burst
with green birds and vitamins.

Because of this
the trees turn in their trenches
and hold up little rain cups
by their slender fingers.
Because of this
a woman stands by her stove
singing and cooking flowers.
Everything here is yellow and green.

Surely spring will allow
a girl without a stitch on
to turn softly in her sunlight
and not be afraid of her bed.
She has already counted seven
blossoms in her green green mirror.
Two rivers combine beneath her.
The face of the child wrinkles
in the water and is gone forever.
The woman is all that can be seen
in her animal loveliness.
Her cherished and obstinate skin
lies deeply under the watery tree.
Everything is altogether possible
and the blind men can also see.

Just Once

Just once I knew what life was for.
In Boston, quite suddenly, I understood;
walked there along the Charles River,
watched the lights copying themselves,
all neoned and strobe-hearted, opening
their mouths as wide as opera singers;
counted the stars, my little campaigners,
my scar daisies, and knew that I walked my love
on the night green side of it and cried
my heart to the eastbound cars and cried
my heart to the westbound cars and took
my truth across a small humped bridge
and hurried my truth, the charm of it, home
and hoarded these constants into morning
only to find them gone.

Again and Again and Again

You said the anger would come back
just as the love did.

I have a black look I do not
like. It is a mask I try on.
I migrate toward it and its frog
sits on my lips and defecates.
It is old. It is also a pauper.
I have tried to keep it on a diet.
I give it no unction.

There is a good look that I wear
like a blood clot. I have
sewn it over my left breast.
I have made a vocation of it.
Lust has taken plant in it
and I have placed you and your
child at its milk tip.

Oh the blackness is murderous
and the milk tip is brimming
and each machine is working
and I will kiss you when
I cut up one dozen new men
and you will die somewhat,
again and again.

You All Know the Story
of the Other Woman

It's a little Walden.
She is private in her breathbed
as his body takes off and flies,
flies straight as an arrow.
But it's a bad translation.
Daylight is nobody's friend.
God comes in like a landlord
and flashes on his brassy lamp.
Now she is just so-so.
He puts his bones back on,
turning the clock back an hour.
She knows flesh, that skin balloon,
the unbound limbs, the boards,
the roof, the removable roof.
She is his selection, part time.
You know the story too! Look,
when it is over he places her,
like a phone, back on the hook.

Moon Song, Woman Song

I am alive at night.
I am dead in the morning,
an old vessel who used up her oil,
bleak and pale boned.
No miracle. No dazzle.
I'm out of repair
but you are tall in your battle dress
and I must arrange for your journey.
I was always a virgin,
old and pitted.
Before the world was, I was.

I have been oranging and fat,
carrot colored, gaped at,
allowing my cracked o's to drop on the sea
near Venice and Mombasa.
Over Maine I have rested.
I have fallen like a jet into the Pacific.
I have committed perjury over Japan.
I have dangled my pendulum,
my fat bag, my gold, gold,
blinkedy light
over you all.

So if you must inquire, do so.
After all I am not artificial.
I looked long upon you,
love-bellied and empty,
flipping my endless display
for you, you my cold, cold
coverall man.

You need only request
and I will grant it.
It is virtually guaranteed
that you will walk into me like a barracks.
So come cruising, come cruising,
you of the blast off,
you of the bastion,
you of the scheme.
I will shut my fat eye down,
headquarters of an area,
house of a dream.

The Ballad of
the Lonely Masturbator

The end of the affair is always death.
She's my workshop. Slippery eye,
out of the tribe of myself my breath
finds you gone. I horrify
those who stand by. I am fed.
At night, alone, I marry the bed.

Finger to finger, now she's mine.
She's not too far. She's my encounter.
I beat her like a bell. I recline
in the bower where you used to mount her.
You borrowed me on the flowered spread.
At night, alone, I marry the bed.

Take for instance this night, my love,
that every single couple puts together
with a joint overturning, beneath, above,
the abundant two on sponge and feather,
kneeling and pushing, head to head.
At night, alone, I marry the bed.

I break out of my body this way,
an annoying miracle. Could I
put the dream market on display?
I am spread out. I crucify.
My little plum is what you said.
At night, alone, I marry the bed.

Then my black-eyed rival came.
The lady of water, rising on the beach,
a piano at her fingertips, shame
on her lips and a flute's speech.
And I was the knock-kneed broom instead.
At night, alone, I marry the bed.

She took you the way a woman takes
a bargain dress off the rack
and I broke the way a stone breaks.
I give back your books and fishing tack.
Today's paper says that you are wed.
At night, alone, I marry the bed.

The boys and girls are one tonight.
They unbutton blouses. They unzip flies.
They take off shoes. They turn off the light.
The glimmering creatures are full of lies.
They are eating each other. They are overfed.
At night, alone, I marry the bed.

Loving me with m
means loving my l
sweet dears, as good
and my feet, those tv
let out to play naked.
my toes. No longer bo
And what's more, see
prehensile joints of joi
all ten stages, root by r
All spirited and wild, tl
piggy went to market an
stayed. Long brown legs and long brown toes.
Further up, my darling, the woman
is calling her secrets, little houses,
little tongues that tell you.

There is no one else but us
in this house on the land spit.
The sea wears a bell in its navel.
And I'm your barefoot wench for a
whole week. Do you care for salami?
No. You'd rather not have a scotch?
No. You don't really drink. You do
drink me. The gulls kill fish,
crying out like three-year-olds.
The surf's a narcotic, calling out,
I am, I am, I am
all night long. Barefoot,
I drum up and down your back.
In the morning I run from door to door
of the cabin playing *chase me*.
Now you grab me by the ankles.
Now you work your way up the legs
and come to pierce me at my hunger mark.

nsideration all your loveliness
ou burn your bootsoles and your
d? How can you sit there saying yes
r? You'll be a pauper when you die, sore
y. Dead, while I still live at our address.
Oh my brother, why do you keep making plans
when I am at seizures of hearts and hands?
Come dance the dance, the Papa-Mama dance;
bring costumes from the suitcase pasted *Île de France*,
the S.S. *Gripsholm*. Papa's London Harness case
he took abroad and kept in our attic laced
with old leather straps for storage and his
scholar's robes, black licorice — that metamorphosis
with its crimson hood. Remember we played costume —
bride black and black, black, black the groom?

Taking into consideration all your loveliness,
the mad hours where once we danced on the sofa
screaming Papa, Papa, Papa, me in my dress,
my nun's habit and you black as a hammer, a bourgeois
priest who kept leaping and leaping and leaping,
Oh brother, Mr. Gunman, why were you weeping,
inventing curses for your sister's pink, pink ear?
Taking aim and then, as usual, being sincere,
saying something dangerous, something egg-spotted
like *I love you*, ignoring the room where we danced,
ignoring the gin that could get us honestly potted,
and crying Mama, Mama, Mama, that old romance:
I tell you the dances we had were really enough,
your hands on my breast and all that sort of stuff.

Remember the yellow leaves that October day
when we married the tree hut and I didn't go away?
Now I sit here burying the attic and all of your
loveliness. If I jump on the sofa you just sit
in the corner and then you just bang on the door.
YOU WON'T REMEMBER! Yes, Mr. Gunman, that's it!
Isn't the attic familiar? Doesn't the season
trample your mind? War, you say. War, you reason.
Please Mr. Gunman, dance one more, commenting
on costumes, holding them to your breast, lamenting
our black love and putting on that Papa dress.
Papa and Mama did so. Can we do less?

Now

See. The lamp is adjusted. The ash tray
was carelessly broken by the maid.
Still, balloons saying *love me, love me*
float up over us on the ceiling.
Morning prayers were said as we sat
knee to knee. Four kisses for that!
And why in hell should we mind
the clock? Turn me over from twelve
to six. Then you taste of the ocean.
One day you huddled into a grief ball,
hurled into the corner like a schoolboy.
Oh come with your hammer, your leather
and your wheel. Come with your needle point.
Take my looking glass and my wounds
and undo them. Turn off the light and
then we are all over black paper.

Now it is time to call attention
to our bed, a forest of skin
where seeds burst like bullets.
We are in our room. We are in
a shoe box. We are in a blood box.
We are delicately bruised, yet we
are not old and not stillborn.
We are here on a raft, exiled from dust.
The earth smell is gone. The blood
smell is here and the blade and its bullet.
Time is here and you'll go his way.
Your lung is waiting in the death market.
Your face beside me will grow indifferent.

Darling, you will yield up your belly and be
cored like an apple. The leper will come
and take our names and change the calendar.
The shoemaker will come and he will rebuild
this room. He will lie on your bed
and urinate and nothing will exist.
Now it is time. Now!

Us

I was wrapped in black
fur and white fur and
you undid me and then
you placed me in gold light
and then you crowned me,
while snow fell outside
the door in diagonal darts.
While a ten-inch snow
came down like stars
in small calcium fragments,
we were in our own bodies
(that room that will bury us)
and you were in my body
(that room that will outlive us)
and at first I rubbed your
feet dry with a towel
because I was your slave
and then you called me princess.
Princess!

Oh then
I stood up in my gold skin
and I beat down the psalms
and I beat down the clothes
and you undid the bridle
and you undid the reins
and I undid the buttons,
the bones, the confusions,
the New England postcards,
the January ten o'clock night,
and we rose up like wheat,
acre after acre of gold,
and we harvested,
we harvested.

Mr. Mine

Notice how he has numbered the blue veins
in my breast. Moreover there are ten freckles.
Now he goes left. Now he goes right.
He is building a city, a city of flesh.
He's an industrialist. He has starved in cellars
and, ladies and gentlemen, he's been broken by iron,
by the blood, by the metal, by the triumphant
iron of his mother's death. But he begins again.
Now he constructs me. He is consumed by the city.
From the glory of boards he has built me up.
From the wonder of concrete he has molded me.
He has given me six hundred street signs.
The time I was dancing he built a museum.
He built ten blocks when I moved on the bed.
He constructed an overpass when I left.
I gave him flowers and he built an airport.
For traffic lights he handed out red and green
lollipops. Yet in my heart I am go children slow.

Song for a Lady

On the day of breasts and small hips,
the window pocked with bad rain,
rain coming on like a minister,
we coupled, so sane and insane.
We lay like spoons while the sinister
rain dropped like flies on our lips
and our glad eyes and our small hips.

"The room is so cold with rain," you said
and you, feminine you, with your flower
said novenas to my ankles and elbows.
You are a national product and power.
Oh my swan, my drudge, my dear wooly rose,
even a notary would notarize our bed
as you knead me and I rise like bread.

Knee Song

Being kissed on the back
of the knee is a moth
at the windowscreen and
yes my darling a dot
on the fathometer is
tinkerbelle with her cough
and twice I will give up my
honor and stars will stick
like tacks in the night
yes oh yes yes yes two
little snails at the back
of the knee building bon-
fires something like eye-
lashes something two zippos
striking yes yes yes small
and me maker.

Eighteen Days Without You

As we kissed good-bye
you made a little frown.
Now Christ's lights are
twinkling all over town.
The cornstalks are broken
in the field, broken and brown.
The pond at the year's end
turns her gray eyelid down.
Christ's lights are
twinkling all over town.

A cat-green ice spreads
out over the front lawn.
The hemlocks are the only
young thing left. You are gone.
I hibernated under the covers
last night, not sleeping until dawn
came up like twilight and the oak leaves
whispered like money, those hangers on.
The hemlocks are the only
young thing left. You are gone.

DECEMBER 2ND

I slept last night
under a bird's shadow
dreaming of nuthatches at the feeder,
jailed to its spine, jailed right
down to the toes, waiting for slow
death in the hateful December snow.
Mother's death came in the spotlight
and mother slamming the door when I need her
and you at the door yesterday,
you at the loss, grown white,
saying what lovers say.

But in my dream
you were a weird stone man
who sleepwalked in, whose features did not change,
your mouth sewn like a seam,
a dressmaker's dummy who began
without legs and a caved-in waist, my old puritan.
You were all muslin, a faded cream
and I put you in six rooms to rearrange
your doors and your thread popped and spoke,
ripping out an uncovered scream
from which I awoke.

Then I took a pill to sleep again
and I was a criminal in solitary,
both cripple and crook
who had picked ruby eyes from men.

One-legged I became and then
you dragged me off by your Nazi hook.
I was the piece of bad meat they made you carry.
I was bruised. You could not miss.
Dreaming gives one such bad luck
and I had ordered this.

This is the mole-
gray mouth of the year.
Yesterday I stole
out to your hunter's cabin-studio,
surprising two woodchucks and a deer
outside our makeshift bungalow.

On the way to Groton
I saw a dead rabbit
in the road, rotten
with crows pecking at his green entrails.
It's nature, you would have said from habit
and continued on to cocktails.

The sun dogs were
in the sky overhead.
You, my voyager,
were dogging up the old globe going west
and I was at the feeder where juncos fed.
Alone in our place I was a guest.

DECEMBER 4TH

And where did we meet?
Was it in London on Carnaby Street?
Was it in Paris on the Left Bank?
That *there* that I can thank?

No. It was Harvard Square
at the kiosk with both of us crying.
I can thank that *there* —
the day Jack Kennedy was dying.

And one hour later he was dead.
The brains fell out of his dazzling head.
And we cried and drank our whiskey straight
and the world remembers the date, the date.

And we both wrote poems we couldn't write
and cried together the whole long night
and fell in love with a delicate breath
on the eve that great men call for death.

DECEMBER 5TH

That was Oswald's November
four long years ago.
I remember
meeting secretly once a week or oftener,
knowing it wrong, but having those reasons.
So I commute to your studio,
my smoothsmith, my softener.
We take love in all its seasons.

This is the last picture page
of the calendar.
Now I feel my age,
watching the feverish birds outside
pocketing grain in their beaks.
The wind is bizarre.
The wind goes *boo, boo, boo* at my side
and the kitchen faucet leaks.

This is the last leaf
in the year's book.
Now I come to grief
as the earth's breast goes hard and mean
and hay is packed for the manger.
Down by the brook
frogs freeze like chessmen and can't be seen
and you are gone, my stranger.

DECEMBER 6TH

A light rain, as tranquil as an apple, today . . .
mild and supple and fat and fullblown sweet
like the last February 2nd on Groundhog Day.
He wouldn't come out and we lay odds
that his Mickey Mouse nose would greet
us, that his coma wasn't part of the gods.

We thought he'd show at the Candlemass,
show his Chippewa shadow at eleven a.m.
We thought that coldblooded thing would pass
like a priest with his mouthful of beets
for the emerging mystic and the stratagem
that his wide awake shadow meets.

Pearl Harbor Day.
The cruciform.
No rain last night, but an icestorm.
Jewels! Today each twig is important,
each ring, each infection, each form
is all that the gods must have meant.

Pearl Harbor Day
leaves scars.
Silver flies in the wind, little stars,
little eye pennies pock up and pock up
and the broken mirrors scatter far
and all the watch parts fill my cup.

Each rock is news.
Each has arrived.
The birds, those beggars, are hardly alive,
feathers like stone and the sealed in food.
Owls force mice into the open. Owls thrive.
The ice will do the birds in, or come unglued.

DECEMBER 8TH

In winter without you I send
a Florida postcard to myself
to somehow remind me of the week
after mid-July and towards the end
when scummy Dog Days were on the shelf
and we had a week of our own to spend.

Snakes snapped their venom
and leftover sparklers were lit
and Roman dogs sniffed the milkweed
from which fertile perfume had come.
Small blackcaps came bit by bit
and we came too, from our need.

The sumac had red heads on display
and the good blood moved into every lamb,
tomatoes and snap beans under Sirius,
field corn and field mice came to stay.
Mornings I washed our plates of egg and jam.
Our last light a whippoorwill spoke to us.

Two years ago, Reservist,
you would have burned
your draft card or
else have gone A.W.O.L.
But you stayed to serve
the Air Force. Your head churned
with bad solutions, carrying
your heart like a football
to the goal, your good heart
that never quite ceases
to know its wrong. From
Frisco you made a phone call.
Next they manufactured you
into an Aero-medic
who placed together
shot off pieces
of men. Some were sent off
too dead to be sick.

But I wrote no diary
for that time then
and you say what you
do today is worse.
Today you unload the bodies of men
out at Travis Air Force
Base — that curse —
no trees, a crater
surrounded by hills.
The Starlifter from
Vietnam, the multi-hearse
jets in. One hundred
come day by day

just forty-eight hours
after death, filled
sometimes with as
many as sixty coffins in array.

Manual Minus Number
Sixteen Handbook
prefers to call this
the human remains.

This is the stand
that the world took
with the enemy's children
and the enemy's gains.
You unload them slipping
in their rubber sacks
within an aluminum coffin —
those human remains,
always the head higher
than the ten little toes.
They are priority when
they are shipped back
with four months pay
and a burial allotment
that they enclose.

All considerations
for these human remains!
They must have an escort!
They are classified!
Never jettisoned in
emergencies from any planes.
Stay aboard! More important
now that they've died.

You say, "You're treated like
shit until you're killed."

And then brought into The Cave,
those stamped human remains
on a Starlifter, a Cargomaster,
a packet, a Hercules
while napalm is in the frying pan,
while napalm is in the death nest.
And what was at home
was The Peace March —
this Washington we seize.

I think today of the animal sounds,
how last night a rebellious fox
was barking out like Lucifer.
When the Beaver Moon lit up the ground
oak twigs scratched like mice in a box.
How in March we waited for the Hyla Crucifer,
those playbell peepers, those one-inch twinkletoes
that come with sticky pads into life when the ice goes.

Mostly it's soundless, the world sealed in,
life turned upside down and down the lock.
So I will remember, remember cicadas in August,
their high whine like a hi-fi, shrill and thin
and when you asked me if I were old enough to darn a sock
I cried and then you held me just as you must
and of course we're not married, we are a pair of scissors
who come together to cut, without towels saying His. Hers.

DECEMBER 11TH

Then I think of you in bed,
your tongue half chocolate, half ocean,
of the houses that you swing into,
of the steel wool hair on your head,
of your persistent hands and then
how we gnaw at the barrier because we are two.

How you come and take my blood cup
and link me together and take my brine.
We are bare. We are stripped to the bone
and we swim in tandem and go up and up
the river, the identical river called Mine
and we enter together. No one's alone.

And what of me?
I work each day in my
leotards at the State School
where the retarded are
locked up with hospital techniques.
Always I walk past the hydro-
cephalic doorman on his stool,
a five-year-old who sits
all day and never speaks,
his head like a twenty-five
cent balloon, three times
the regular size. It's nature
but nature works such crimes.

I go to the large cement
day room where fifty kids
are locked up for what
they strangely call play.
The toys are not around,
not given to my invalids
because possessions might get
broken or in the way.
We can't go out. There are no
snowsuits, sometimes no shoes
so what I do for them is what
I bring for them to use.

The room stinks of urine.
Only the two-headed baby
is antiseptic in her crib.
Now I take the autoharp,
the drum, the triangle,

the tambourine and the keys
for locked doors and locked
sounds, blind and sharp.
We have clapping of hands
and stamping of feet, please.
I play my humming and lullaby
sounds for each disease.

I sing *The Fox Came Out
on a Chilly Night*
and Bobby, my favorite
Mongoloid, sings Fox to me.
I bring out my silk scarfs
for a group of sprites.
Susan wants the blue scarf
and no one is orderly.
I sway with two red scarfs.
I'm in trance,
calling *love me, woo, woo*
and we all passionately dance.

Remember that day last June
in the month of the Long-Day-Beauty
that is called Indians' *Wawe-Pesin?*
I tell you Summer came not one day too soon
and surely the calendar did its duty
and we stayed a weekend at the Provincetown Inn.

Remember that thunder storm in July
when the lightning came down the hill —
and I wore my sneakers to stay brave —
came rolling down like a beach ball to fry
and hang inside of the outdoor stone grill,
a toy fire that wouldn't behave?

Remember that barhopping hunt
for a good whiskey and a straight rye,
The Old Overholt with a picture of Washington
looking somewhat constipated on the front
or The Wild Turkey with the crossed eyes —
bourbon we tossed down until we were numb?

DECEMBER 14TH

The migratory birds
have flown the coop
but they'll be back
with their built-in compass.
They'll come back the way
the circus does each year —
with aerialists, our angular
birds that loop the loop.
Two years ago you bought
seats for the children in us.
*Children of all ages
the ninety-sixth season is here!*

La Toria held by her
wrist to a skyward rope
executed upwards of one
hundred body turns.
The lions in their cruel
cages marched up and down.
And FIREMAN SAVE MY CHILD
let midgets bring us hope,
scurrying to the scene, toy
engines while the toy fire burned.
On the outside, two days before
someone murdered a clown.

The ceiling was strung
up with tenement laundry.
A clown tied a bib on a lion
and fed him like a baby.
Ponies dressed like camels,
poodles dressed like whores

61

and Doval The Great with his
precious toes (I didn't want to see)
climbed up over the elephants
and the children into immortality.
And you had your pocket picked,
my boyish conspirator.

DECEMBER 15TH

The day of the lonely drunk
is here. No weather reports,
no fox, no birds, no sweet chipmunks,
no sofa game, no summer resorts.

No whatever it was we had,
no sky, no month — just booze.
The half moon is acid, bitter, sad
as I sing the Blended Whiskey Blues.

Once upon a time
you grew up in a bedrom the size of a dime
and shared it with your sister. That was West End
Avenue in Manhattan. Longing for country you were
    penned
into city, peering across the Hudson at Palisades Park.
The boy in you played stickball until it was dark.

Once upon a time
I was the only child forbidden to climb
over the garden wall. I didn't dare to speak
up over the Victorian houseful of rare antiques.
My dolls were all proper, waiting in neat rows.
My room was high ceilinged, lonely and full of echoes.

Once upon a time
you said, "Now that the cabin is ours, I'm
going to run the power in." And we had a power party.
I made gingham curtains. We nailed up your Doctoral
    degree.
We turned the stove on twice. Oh my love, oh my louse,
we make our own electricity while we play house.

Today I bought a Scotch Pine —
O Tannenbaum — a Christmas tree,
as green as a turtle, a forest
of gum and resin and turpentine.
My love, my louse, my absentee,
alone in our place I was not a guest.

With my box from the Five and Dime
I hung bells and balls and silver floss
and one intense strand of reds and greens.
At the end I topped off the ragged pine
with a flashy star, the five point cross
that twinkles for the Nazarene.

Doing this reminded me of the fall awards
we gave to different trees, *First Prize*
was tacked upon the rock maple
in Lincoln Center, then out towards
Weston we pinned *Best Birch at Sunrise*.
We took our census of colors not people.

The purple oaks, the quivering aspens,
those heavy popples the color of old coins;
the woodbine — each with an award on its trunk,
pinned by us with home-made ribbons
on Columbus Day. Prizes when acid joins
the pigment and the sap has been drunk.

Today I bought a sprig of mistletoe,
all warts and leaves and fruit
and stem — the angel of the kiss —
and hung it in our bungalow.
My love, we will take root
during the Christmas Armistice.

DECEMBER 18TH

Swift boomerang, come get!
I am delicate. You've been gone.
The losing has hurt me some, yet
I must bend for you. See me arch. I'm turned on.
My eyes are lawn-colored, my hair brunette.

Kiss the package, Mr. Bind!
Yes? Would you consider hurling yourself
upon me, rigorous but somehow kind?
I am laid out like paper on your cabin kitchen shelf.
So draw me a breast. I like to be underlined.

Look, lout! Say yes!
Draw me like a child. I shall need
merely two round eyes and a small kiss.
A small o. Two earrings would be nice. Then proceed
to the shoulder. You may pause at this.

Catch me. I'm your disease.
Please go slow all along the torso
drawing beads and mouths and trees
and o's, a little *graffiti* and a small *hello*
for I grab, I nibble, I lift, I please.

Draw me good, draw me warm.
Bring me your raw-boned wrist and your
strange, Mr. Bind, strange stubborn horn.
Darling, bring with this an hour of undulations, for
this is the music for which I was born.

Lock in! Be alert, my acrobat
and I will be soft wood and you the nail
and we will make fiery ovens for Jack Sprat
and you will hurl yourself into my tiny jail
and we will take a supper together and that
will be that.